Studies in Governance and Politics

ISBN-13 978-0615584850
ISBN-10 0615584853

Also by Kevin R. Kosar

Failing Grades: The Federal Politics of Education Standards

Editor, *Bridging the Gap: Higher Education and Career-Centered Welfare Reform*

Editor, the Federal Education Policy History website

Ronald Reagan and Education Policy

Contents

Preface

Scholars have given little attention to President Ronald Reagan's education policy agenda and record. This short introductory study begins to redress this dearth by assessing the Reagan administration's kindergarten through high school (K-12) education policy record.

It argues that Reagan won a few early policy victories and then suffered many defeats. Reagan entered the presidency promising to return the responsibility for schooling back to states and localities. Ironically, Reagan ended up both expanding and legitimizing the federal role in schooling.

The turning point occurred when the Reagan administration released *A Nation At Risk*, a report declaring a national student achievement crisis. The report garnered immense media coverage and stoked the perception that America's schools were failing. Great Communicator though he was, Reagan proved unable to sell a reduced federal role in schooling as the cure for the national education malaise.

Ultimately, Reagan felt sufficient political pressure that he campaigned as an education reformer, and signed laws that increased federal education spending and established new programs.

1

A Planned and Orderly Transfer Back

Ronald W. Reagan was not an ideologue, at least not on the issue of the federal government's role in schooling. As in many other areas of policy, Reagan had ideas about what was right and sensible and what was not. Collectively, his viewpoint was an amalgam of middle American conservatism, libertarianism, dual federalism, and nostalgia for simpler times.(1)

As a candidate, Reagan made clear his education policy philosophy. Reagan believed that parents—not government—had the primary responsibility for their children's moral upbringing and education.(2) He thought children needed strict discipline, and solid training in the "three R's"—reading, writing, and arithmetic.

Reagan greatly admired private schools, especially religious ones. Private schools, he thought, were good in and of themselves, and he esteemed them all the more for being alternatives for parents dissatisfied with their communities' public schools.(3) Reagan also thought private schools provided healthy competition for public schools—spurs to improvement. Accordingly, Reagan felt government should not throw up any impediments to the formation and operation of private schools. And, critically, he wanted private schools to remain just that—private. Government should not attempt to influence their operations or curricula.

Finally, Reagan believed schools should remain the creatures of their local communities and home states. He believed the federal and state governments have separate spheres of activity that are defined by the Constitution.(4) The Tenth Amendment reads, "The powers not delegated to the United States by the Constitution, nor prohibited by it to the States, are reserved to the States respectively, or to the people." Reagan observed correctly that the federal government had greatly expanded its sphere of authority over the past century, taking up areas of public policy that had traditionally belonged to the states. Reagan wanted to reverse that trend. Not only was it the constitutionally legitimate thing to do, but he also felt the federal government had not been successful in many of the areas it usurped.

As a candidate, he repeatedly said that he wanted to shrink the federal government's authority over schooling and return power to states and localities. In 1979, Reagan made his position quite clear in a statement to the press,

"The founding fathers created a federation of sovereign states and intended that these states maintain as much power as possible. This is the meaning of the 10th article of the Bill of Rights. And I think what has happened is that the federal government has slowly usurped this power. I propose a planned and orderly transfer back."(5)

~

2

Early Victories, 1981 to 1982

While the President himself was not an ideologue, many of his most powerful supporters and top aides were, and, they provided Reagan with specific policy ideas. Two documents, the Republican Party Platform of 1980 and the Heritage Foundation's *Mandate for Leadership*,(6) express the ideas of these "movement conservatives' and provided a blueprint for the policy initiatives they wanted Reagan to advance. The "new right" had roots in the 1964 presidential campaign of Barry Goldwater. They sought to rework the federal government dramatically by making it smaller (the military being a rare exception), less intrusive in the market, and less onerous on individuals.(7)   Private initiative was to be encouraged; wealth equalization and deependence upon the federal government was to be discouraged. Liberty came first, and equality, depending on how one defined it, came second.(8)

In terms of education, both the Republican Party Platform and *Mandate for Leadership* sounded an alarmist note. The platform described a United States that was "adrift." Its economy was feeble, its influence abroad waning, and the "aspirations of [its] people" were "being smothered." The platform's education plank stated,

"Next to religious training and the home, education is the most important means by which families hand down to each new generation their ideals and beliefs. It is a pillar of a free society. But today, parents are losing control of their children's schooling. The Democratic Congress and its counterparts in many states have launched one fad after another, building huge new bureaucracies to misspend our taxes. The result has been a shocking decline in student performance, lack of basics in the classroom, forced busing [of black students into predominately white schools and vice versa], teacher strikes, and manipulative and sometime amoral indoctrination."(9)

It called for replacing the "crazy quilt of wasteful [education] programs with a system of block grants that will restore decision-making to local officials responsible to voters and parents." The Republican platform stated that "learning is the highway to equal opportunity." It declared that "America has a stake in maintaining standards of high quality in education," but it did not propose federal policies to achieve this goal. The Platform advocated an end to the busing of students, a lower federal share of schools spending, and an end to the "regulatory vendetta" by the Internal Revenue Service against private schools.(10) The platform called for Congress to "restore the right of individuals to participate in voluntary, nondenominational prayer in schools and other public facilities" and for tuition tax credits, which would "compensate parents" who pay to send their children to private schools.(11)

Mandate for Leadership expressed a similar viewpoint of schooling in the United States.(12) It derided the Department of Education (herein "the Department"), which was created in 1979,(13) as little more than a payoff by the Democratic Party to the National Education Association, the influential teachers union.(14) *Mandate for Leadership* stated that the federal government should limit its role in education to (1) information gathering and dissemination, (2) consultation and technical assistance to schools, and (3) educational research and development. *Mandate* cast the Department as an oppressive, poorly administered bureaucracy that usurped local control through a "labyrinth of prescriptive programs," some of which had been captured by "ideological militants" who used the Department's power to promote secularism, nihilism, and other radical ideas in public schools.(15) As federal education spending on these pernicious programs had increased, so had the Department's control over schools. The result was a plunge in student test scores.

Thus, *Mandate* argued, the Department should be replaced with a lesser office or entity, and its programs should be cut back. Where possible, education programs kept should be sent to other federal departments or consolidated under block grants so that discretion for the spending of federal dollars would return to states and localities. It advocated assessing all federal education programs for their ability to improve children's skills in reading, writing, and mathematics. *Mandate for Leadership* also promoted enactment of private school tuition tax credits, and ending busing of students for racial purposes. Were the Reagan administration to do these things, it could sound the "death-knell for statist education."

In its first year, the administration held back on pushing new education policies, such as tuition tax credits for parents who sent their children to privately-operated schools. New programs would not fit with its overall domestic program—supply-side economics. Reagan had been elected, in part, because of widespread public dissatisfaction with the economy. Inflation was over 12 percent and the prime interest rate climbed above 20 percent.(16) To spur economic growth, the supply-side economic program required cutting government spending and taxes. Many in Congress were aghast when Reagan proposed, in February of 1981, to slice over $35 billion from the Carter-proposed 1982 budget. Many in Congress also were, quite probably, even more disturbed to learn that the American public, when polled, favored spending cuts.(17) Reagan upped the ante in March, pushing the proposed cuts to $60 billion, almost 9.3 percent of the budget.(18)

The supply-side program put the Department and federal education programs on the chopping block. David Stockman, Director of the Office of Management and Budget (OMB), was given great discretion over crafting the President's 1982 budget proposal. He wanted federal education programs cut 40% to 100%.(19) But cuts of such a magnitude were not politically possible, so he set his sights lower—education spending would be trimmed 22.5%, from $16.9 billion (1981) to $13.1 billion (1982). There were no sacred education cows—even the previously untouchable compensatory education programs for the poor and nonwhite were to be reduced 20 percent.(20)

And Stockman and the administration proposed rolling 50 education programs into two new block grants. This would dramatically reduce federal discretion over these programs. Devolving authority also would give the Reagan administration a good argument for laying off the employees who administered these programs. Downsizing the Department's employee cohort would reduce costs and be an important step in dismantling the agency. Furthermore, the Reagan administration hoped that block grants would shut off funding to the left-wing grantees (e.g., academics and activist groups) whom they found objectionable. The presumption was that if given the freedom, states and local education agencies likely would not use federal funds for the precise purposes stipulated previously by the categorical grants. They would put the money to more productive educational purposes.

Reagan's gambit worked—partially. After grueling negotiations his budget got through Congress and reached his desk for signing in August of 1981. Fourty-four education programs were subsumed into the block grants, including the categorical grant program that provided funding for busing students for the purpose of racial integration.(21) The previous year (1981), the Department had $17 billion to spend. In 1981, the Department would have $14.7 billion $14.5 billion, a significant reduction in a time of high inflation.

With devolution of federal power to the states begun, Reagan could now turn to further downsizing the federal role in schooling and enacting conservative policies. During his campaign for the presidency, Reagan had proposed abolishing the Department of Education. His top aide, Edwin Meese, agreed. According to one observer, Meese thought the Department was a "great, bureaucratic joke."(22) In autumn of 1982, the administration began to advance its education policies. Reagan spoke out in favor of abolishing the Department, said that the Supreme Court had erred in its rulings against teacher-led prayer in the classrooms, and criticized the busing of children to achieve racial integration.(23) Over the next year and one half, the administration unleashed a flurry of education proposals, which, if enacted, would dramatically alter the federal role in schooling. Its proposals included:

· Replacing the Department with a foundation to administer some federal education programs (the rest would be dispersed to other departments;

· Enacting a constitutional amendment to permit student prayer in schools;

· Enacting tuition tax credits for parents who sent their children to private schools;

• Encouraging the growth of the number of private schools by allowing more of them to claim tax-exempt status;

• Creating an experimental program that would allow students in Title I programs to claim their share of Title I aid and use it as a voucher to attend a school of choice; and

• Subsuming more education programs into block grants.(24)

Also, there was the critical matter of money. To reduce the federal role in schooling, the administration had to cut federal spending. In his 1983 budget, Reagan proposed more big cuts in spending authority. The administration estimated that the Department had spent $3.1 billion on elementary, secondary, and vocational education in 1981. The plan was to chop this down more each year—to $1.9 billion in 1983 and $1.5 billion in 1984 and 1985. The Department, or its successor entity, would have its budget reduced by over 40% (not accounting for inflation) between 1981 and 1985.(25) This would be part and parcel of the "planned and orderly transfer back" to the states of control over the schools.

President Reagan faced a Congress partially in his favor. The new Congress, which began in January of 1983, featured a Senate where Republicans outnumbered Democrats 54 to 46. The House of Representatives, though, posed a huge stumbling block for the administration. The Democratic Party held a 269 to 165 majority. Especially problematic was the House's committee of jurisdiction for education. It was dominated by liberal Democrats. The House Committee on Education and Labor had 20 Democrats to 16 Republicans, and the top three Democrats included Carl Perkins (KY), Augustus Hawkins (CA), and William D. Ford (MI). All three were long-serving members who supported Great Society-type, redistributive federal programs.(26) To these men, the central problem of schooling was money; schools attended by poor and nonwhite children had too little.(27)

While the House posed a formidable challenge, Reagan might be able to overcome it if he had public support for his education policies. Despite these members of Congress, the Reagan administration had forced through a budget that had ended 44 federal education programs. Could Reagan do it again?

3

The April Surprise: A Nation at Risk, 1983

In early January of 1981, President-Elect Reagan's staff vetted possible candidates for Secretary of Education. Terrel H. Bell's name came up, possibly at the suggestion of incoming Secretary of Defense, Caspar Weinberger.(28)

Bell had previously served in the Office of Education. In short order, he was nominated and appointed to the position. Though a Republican, Bell did not agree with the "movement Republicans," who saw little or no role for the federal government in education. Bell thought America's educational institutions were in desperate condition and that someone needed to both preserve a federal role in education and "rally the American people around their schools and colleges."(29) By autumn of 1981, he was annoying the movement conservatives in the administration by disagreeing with OMB director Stockman's proposals for further cuts in education spending.(30)

Bell concluded that he might stoke public interest in repairing the schools by having the federal government craft a report pointing out the condition of American education.(31) Bell's proposal to create a presidentially-appointed commission to study this topic was rebuffed by the White House. So, Bell used his secretarial authority to establish the National Commission on Excellence in Education on August 26, 1981.

In April of 1983, the Commission presented its draft, *A Nation at Risk: The Imperative for Educational Reform* to Bell. Written in terms as alarmist as its title, *A Nation At Risk* described an education system that was rudderless and sinking. The nation had twenty-three million illiterates and test scores had been falling steadily for almost two decades. It declared that the very livelihood of America was threatened by the poor state of the educational system, the foundations of which were being "eroded by a rising tide of mediocrity."

Worse for Reagan was that *A Nation at Risk* did not endorse any of the devolutionary and privatizing policies he was pushing. While the federal role was limited, the report's authors wrote that "we believe the Federal Government's role includes several functions of national consequence that states and localities are unlikely to be able to meet." Among the tasks listed were "supporting curriculum improvement and research on teaching, learning, and the management of schools." It further declared that the "Federal Government has the primary responsibility to identify the national interest in education" and that "educational excellence costs, but in the long run, mediocrity costs far more."(32)

Bell forwarded the report to President Reagan, who apparently did not read it, but kept to his promise to hold a press conference on it. (33)

On April 26th, 1983 President Reagan spoke before a heavily attended conference in the State Dining Room of the White House. He agreed that the state of the schools and colleges was poor. Reagan quoted Jefferson dictum that "If a nation expects to be ignorant and free, it expects what never was and never will be." He then attempted to hitch these finding to his roll-back agenda—

"We spent more on education at all levels than any other country in the world. But what have we bought with all that spending? I was interested to see...the almost uninterrupted decline in student achievement scores during the past two decades, decades in which the Federal presence in education grew and grew."(34)

The President then claimed that the best federal policy response was educational vouchers, school prayer, and tuition tax cuts for parents who send their children to private schools. Reagan's message was clear—the crisis should be handled by parents and localities, and the federal government ought to reduce its detrimental meddling in the public schools.

That night, United Press International's newswire carried a piece on the report, "Panel Backs More—and Harder—School Work."(35) Major media, including the *New York Times*, *Washington Post*, *MacNeil Lehrer Report*, and *Associated Press* seized upon the report. Within the next few weeks, hundreds of newspapers reported *A Nation at Risk*'s grim findings on American education. David Gergen, presidential assistant for communications, said, "The report just took off in the media."(36) Over 100,000 copies of *A Nation at Risk* were distributed before the end of May.(37)

~

4

The Great Communicator Struggles, 1983

Ronald Reagan often has been called "the great communicator." He had an uncanny ability to deliver powerful speeches, speeches that profoundly stirred the media and the public. He was known for tossing off crowd-wowing quips. Yet, for all his rhetorical prowess, President Reagan had a difficult time framing the results of *A Nation At Risk* to comport with his goal to diminish the federal role in schooling.

The administration utilized a political consulting firm to help it devise a response to the intense media attention to *A Nation At Risk*. The firm examined the public's attitudes on education and devised talking points for Reagan. It "found favorable public responses to some ideas in [*A Nation At Risk*] that fit Reagan's philosophy: tougher educational standards, more school discipline, emphasis on basic courses, and teacher accountability." Reagan's advisers then attempted to align Reagan "with the report and sidetrack obvious pressures for more federal funding for education.(38)

To this end, Reagan toured the country with Bell and delivering speeches

that decried the condition of education, the most obvious effect of which
was to further fuel the public's sense that there was a crisis in education.
He emphasized a "back to the basics" message and insisted that more
federal involvement and spending were not the answers to the
problem.(39) The administration began to talk less of abolishing the
Department of Education. In June 1983 a reporter asked White House
spokesman Larry Speakes whether the President still intended to abolish
the Department. "Obviously it could be very difficult legislatively. It
hasn't come up," Speakes responded.(40) By the year's end, Reagan had
shelved the idea.(41) To the confusion of observers and the dismay of
conservatives, Reagan stumped for increased federal spending to improve
student learning in science. Congress was more than happy to oblige, and
enacted this legislation the next year (P.L. 98-377). In his 1984 general
election campaign against Walter Mondale, Reagan stumped for education
reform.(42)

The administration also eased out Terrel Bell and appointed William J.
Bennett as Secretary of Education. The conservative former Secretary of
the National Endowment for the Humanities used his bully pulpit to
promote his education ideas. Bennett churned out a series of reports
calling for better schools.(43) *First Lessons* said that elementary school
children ought to learn "the basic facts and understandings of our
civilization." *American Education: Making It Work* (1988) argued that
curricular content needed to be strengthened and higher student

achievement encouraged. Yet, Bennett, like Reagan, did not suggest that these goals could be achieved through federal education policies.

"What is to be done? Government has a role here—especially state and local authorities, which oversee our public schools; and the federal government has an important part to play as well—through speeches, reports, recommendations, through the dissemination of ideas and the setting of a national agenda, through funding for various enterprises. Individuals have an even more central role—at home, and in voluntary associations. But above all, we as a society, as a common culture, have to respond to the call of national history, and to the responsibility it imposes upon us of instilling in our children an informed appreciation of American principles and American practices."(44)

Bennett stuck to Reagan's message—the federal government was not the answer to the crisis.

Yet, for all these efforts to align Reagan with *A Nation At Risk*, President Reagan's message of less spending and less federal involvement did not take with the press or public. There was a basic dissonance in the logic. A federal government report and the President of the United States had declared that America faced a national crisis in schooling. Yet, Reagan argued that America's federal government, which is supposed to "promote the general welfare" and contend with "great and national interests," must to decrease its role in the schools.(45) Additionally, it was far from obvious how the policies he advocated—tuition tax credits, prayer in the schools, block grants, and less federal spending— would help bolster U.S. students' achievement. The administration's argument simply did not make obvious sense to the public or the press.

At the April 26th press conference on *A Nation At Risk*, Reagan had pointed out that a 1982 Gallup poll found the majority of those surveyed thought "Washington should exert less influence in determining the educational program of the public schools."(46) But after the release of *A Nation At Risk*, polls showed growing public concern for the state of education.(47) In December of 1980, 52 percent of those asked about education spending said America was spending too little. By 1984, that number had increased to 64 percent, and it stayed between 60 and 64 percent through the end of Reagan's term in 1988.(48)

~

5

Defeat, 1984 to 1988

Over the next five years, the Reagan administration had to fight to eke out the smallest education policy victories. It successfully pushed legislation giving religious student groups equal access to use school facilities for school meetings was enacted into law (P.L. 98-377, 1984); it slightly reformed a federal bilingual education program to its liking; and it won a small amount of funding for an experimental school choice program (P.L. 100-297, 1988).(49)

Otherwise, the Reagan administration suffered stinging defeats. When Reagan announced his appointment of Bennett, the Senate hinted that it might refuse to confirm Bennett unless Reagan signed a letter stating that he would not attempt to abolish the Department of Education. Reagan complied, and Bennett was confirmed.(50)

Reagan also was forced to approve legislation that reauthorized aide to school libraries (P.L. 98-280, 1984), the much-loathed by conservatives Women's Equal Education Equity Act (P.L. 98-511, 1984), and increased impact aid (P.L. 100-297, 1988). He even had entirely new education programs enacted on his watch, such as scholarships for teachers and administrators (P.L. 98-588, 1984).(51) The coup de grace came in November of 1986 when the Democrats won of control of the Senate. Reagan's push for conservative education policies would be stymied by the Democratic Congress.

Perhaps most significantly, the Reagan administration could not roll-back the federal role in K-12 education—not if one measures it in dollars. Reagan's first budget (1982) cut funding below the level of Carter's last budget (1981)—from $17.0 to $14.7 billion. Subsequently, the appropriations process tended to fall into a simple pattern—Reagan would propose spending reductions and program eliminations, Congress would demand higher funding and continued funding for all programs, and the President would strike a compromise. After the hullabaloo set off by *A*

Figure 1. Education Department Outlays (Billions of Dollars)

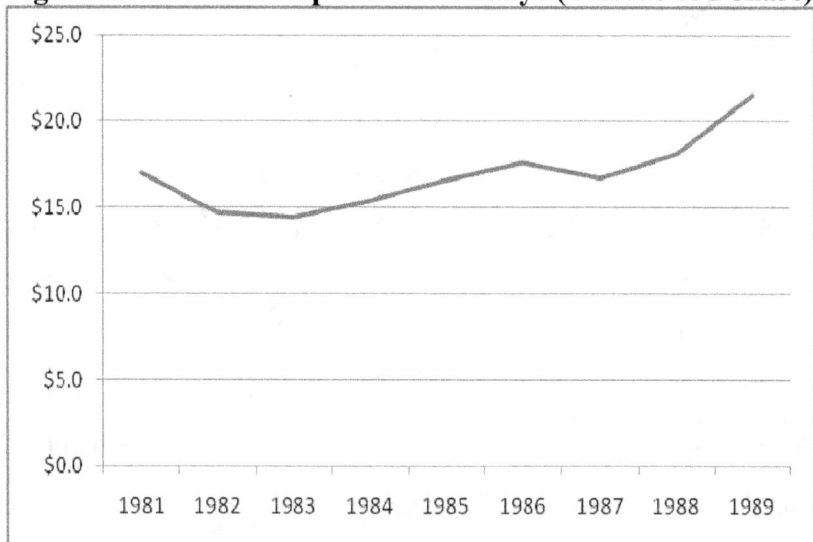

Source: Office of Management and Budget's *Annual Budget of the United States Government*, 1983-1991 and *Fiscal Year 1982 Budget Revisions*.

Nation at Risk in 1983, Reagan could not credibly threaten to veto an education appropriation bill and force a sharp downsizing of the federal role in schooling.(52) All told, during Reagan's time in office education outlays grew from $14.7 billion to $21.5 billion per year—a 46.3% increase. (**Figure 1**) (53)

That said, Reagan did slow the growth of education spending during his terms if one accounts for the high inflation of the period. (Inflation, of course, erodes the purchasing power of money—the buyer gets fewer goods and services for each dollar spent.) Expressed as 1981 dollars, Reagan's 1982 budget cut education spending 18.2%, from $17.0 billion to $13.9 billion. Reagan's education spending record looks very different than the picture displayed in **Figure 1** when one accounts for inflation. (**Figure 2**)

Figure 2. Education Department Outlays Adjusted for Inflation (Billions of Dollars)

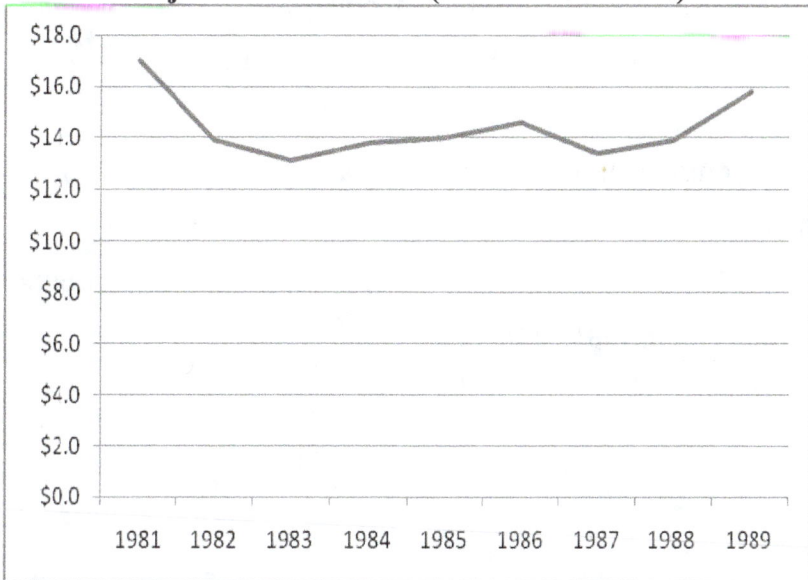

Note: Inflation adjusted by author using Bureau of Labor Statistics data.

In 1981 dollars, education spending increased only 13.7%, from $13.9 billion to $15.8 billion during the Reagan years. (**Figure 2**) But this growth is smaller still when one considers that President Carter's last budget spent $17.0 billion on schooling. Again, in 1981 dollars, going from $17.0 billion in 1981 to $15.8 billion in 1989 is cut of 7.1%. As **Figure 2** shows, Reagan literally bent the education spending curve— twice.

Reagan had a similar experience with the compensatory education spending programs. The Reagan administration thought these programs— which aimed to improve achievement among poor and nonwhite children—were ineffective and ensnared in red tape. It had hoped to cut them back or turn them into voucher or block grant programs. Reagan won sharp cuts twice, but spending on these programs crept back up over time. Compensatory education program outlays were $3.4 billion in 1981, and $4.2 billion in 1989, a 23.5% increase. (**Figure 3**)

Adjusted for inflation, compensatory education spending fell from $3.4 billion in Carter's last budget (1981) to $2.8 billion in Reagan's first budget (1982). At the end of Reagan's second term, it was $3.1 billion, 8.8% lower than in 1981. (**Figure 4**)

Figure 3. Compensatory Education Outlays (Billions of Dollars)

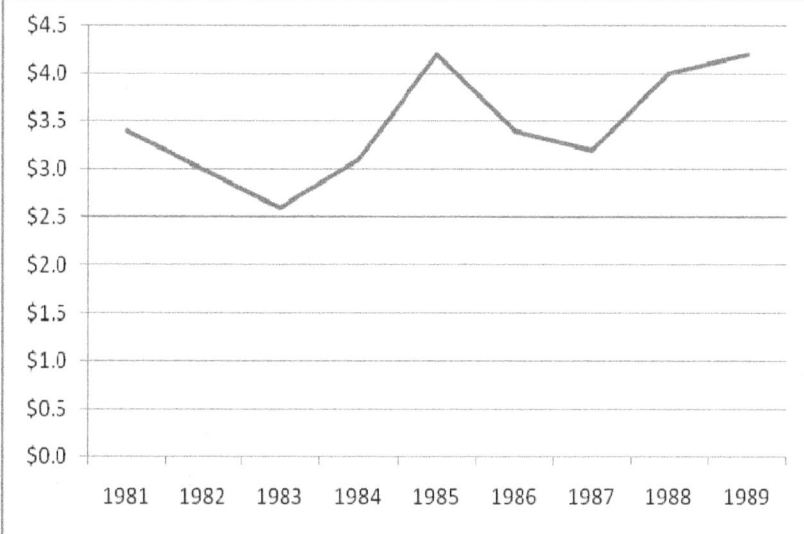

Source: Office of Management and Budget's *Annual Budget of the United States Government*, 1983-1991 and *Fiscal Year 1982 Budget Revisions*.

Figure 4. Compensatory Education Outlays Adjusted for Inflation (Billions of 1981 Dollars)

Source: Inflation adjusted by author using Bureau of Labor Statistics data.

~

6

Conclusion

Ronald Reagan entered the Oval Office hoping to dramatically reduce the federal role in schooling. In his first year and during his first term generally, he won at least two victories—some discretion over federal education dollars was pushed down to the states and the growth of federal spending on schools was slowed.

Though he won these small battles, Reagan clearly lost the war. There was no "planned and orderly transfer back." His administration failed to abolish the Department of Education, enact tuition tax credits, or any of his other preferred policies. And as for spending, in retrospect, the Reagan years were little more than a short-term slowdown. The Department of Education's outlays continue to rise and rise. (**Figure 5** and **Figure 6**)(54) The federal role in education at all levels—preschool, K-12, and post-secondary—keeps growing.

Figure 5. Education Department Outlays (Billions of Dollars)

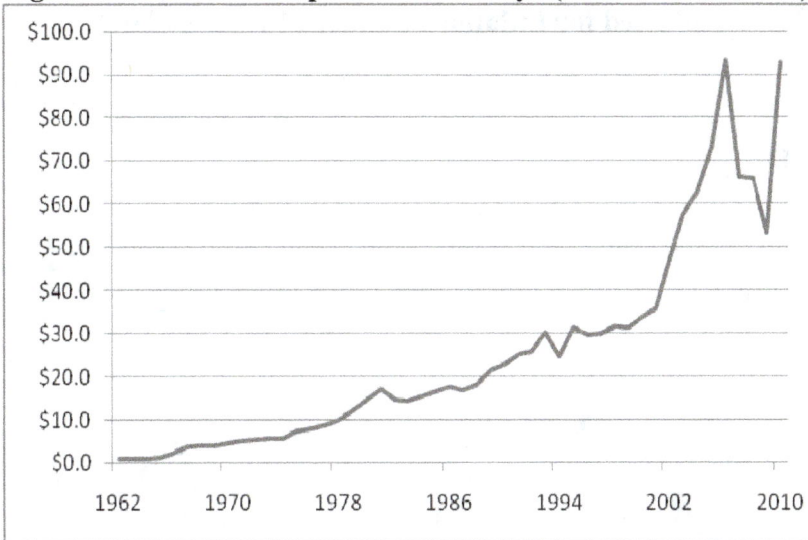

Source: Office of Management and Budget's *Annual Budget of the United States Government*, 2010, Historical Tables, Table 4.1.

Perhaps most profoundly, Reagan was unable to square in the public's mind that a nationwide educational crisis did not require an increased federal role. With "a nation at risk," the public was not especially responsive to talk of the "genius of local control" or the 10th amendment and federalism.

**Figure 6. Education Department Outlays
Adjusted for Inflation (Billions of 1981 Dollars)**

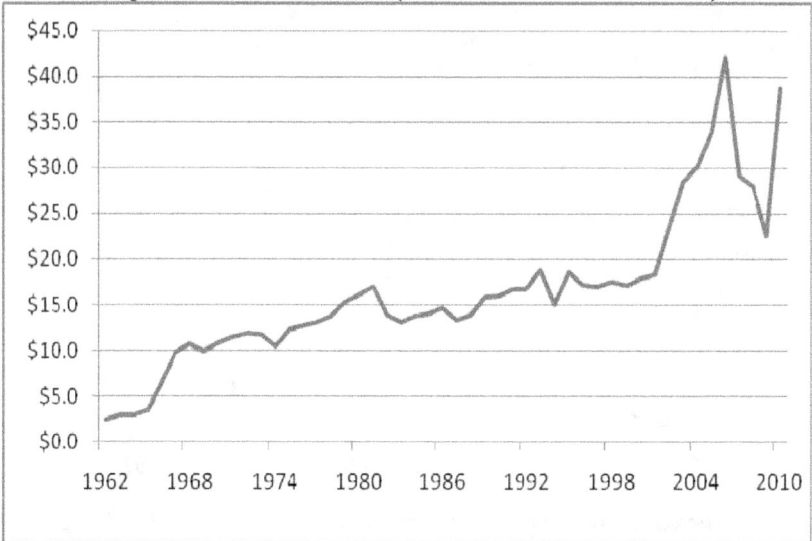

Source: Office of Management and Budget's *Annual Budget of the United States Government*, 2010, Historical Tables, Table 4.1. Inflation adjusted by author using Bureau of Labor Statistics data.

One clear legacy of Reagan's presidency is that student achievement has become the central goal of federal education policy. This was not the case previously, other goals, such as racial integration and equalization of per pupil funding, had been regnant. To this day, both federal and state education policy aims to improve student learning in basic subjects, such as mathematics, reading, and science. Education standards and testing are part of all states education systems and are a sharp focus of federal policy. Newspapers continue to carry articles on the latest test scores.

Conclusion

Reagan's Republican successor, George H.W. Bush, tried to square this circle with his "America 2000," a federal plan that aimed to bolster student achievement through stronger state control. America 2000 confused many observers and very quickly was stalled by a Democratic Congress.(55)

Reagan's failure to shrink the federal role in schooling meant that future Republicans would have to grapple with a basic problem: what should conservative education policy look like? Returning to the old days of "leave it to the states" simply would not fly. Robert Dole in his run for the White House in 1996 tried that message, and it failed terribly.

The next Republican president, George W. Bush, abandoned the conservative small-government position and actively promoted a bigger federal role in schooling in order to improve student achievement.(56) In his first year in office, he signed the No Child Left Behind Act (P.L. 107-110), a law that provided a large increase in federal spending on schools, and which thrust the federal government more deeply into schools' operations and curricula.(57)

~

Endnotes

(1) Catherine A. Lugg, _For God and Country: Conservatism and American School Policy_ (Peter Lang, 1996), pp. 12-15 and 31-35. Lugg also cites "militant anticommunism" as a factor in Reagan's thinking on education. This author's review of the record, though, revealed a very limited influence of anti-communism on Reagan's thinking on education. On nostalgia, see citation 2.

(2) The role of schools, in this view, is to act as agents of parents. Reagan's view echoed one enunciated by the U.S. Supreme Court: "The fundamental theory of liberty upon which all governments in this Union repose excludes any general power of the state to standardize its children by forcing them to accept instruction from public teachers only. The child is not the mere creature of the state; those who nurture him and direct his destiny have the right, coupled with the high duty, to recognize and prepare him for additional obligations." Pierce v. Society of Sisters of the Holy Names of Jesus and Mary 268 U.S. 510 (1925).

(3) Some of these positive feelings for parochial schools may have come from his happy experiences at the small (250 student) Eureka College, a Christian school in Eureka, Illinois. Ronald Reagan, _Where's the Rest of Me?_ (Duell, Sloan and Pearce, 1965), chapters 1-2.

(4) Paul Hendrickson, "Eight Things You Need to Know About Ronald Reagan," _Washington Post_, November 13, 1979, p. B1. The following August, candidate Reagan told the crowd at a fair in Mississippi, "I believe in states' rights." He also noted that if elected president he intended to "restore to state and local government the power that properly

belongs to them." Douglas E. Kneeland, "Reagan Urges Blacks to Look Past Labels and Vote for Him," *New York Times*, August 6, 1980, p. A1.

(5) E.g., The Democratic Congressional Campaign Committee, *The 1980 Campaign Promises of Ronald Reagan* (Washington: DCCC, 1981), 56-57.

(6) Republican National Committee, "Republican Party Platform of 1980" (adopted by the Republican National Convention, July 15, 1980); and Heritage Foundation, *Mandate for Leadership: Policy Management in a Conservative Administration* (Washington: Heritage Foundation, 1980-1981). David Stockman, Reagan's first director of the Office of Management and Budget, stated that *Mandate for Leadership* was used by the administration and helped it to "hit the ground running" upon entering office. One of the authors of the education portion of Mandate for Leadership stated, "I've seen the stuff we gave to Ed Meese [Edwin Meese, II, influential counselor to President Reagan] used line for line." Eileen White, "Power, Visibility Come to Heritage Foundation," *Education Week*, September 28, 1981.

(7) E.g., see the statements of David Stockman and Terrel Bell (Reagan's first secretary of education), and others. David Stockman, *The Triumph of Politics: Why the Reagan Revolution Failed* (Harper & Rowe, 1986); and Terrel Bell, *The Thirteenth Man: A Reagan Cabinet Memoir* (Free Press, 1988).

(8) Their general philosophy was much encapsulated in Reagan's inaugural address of January 20, 1981, in which he stated, The economic ills we suffer have come upon us over several decades [....] In this present crisis, government is not the solution to our problem [....] It is no coincidence that our present troubles parallel and are proportionate to the intervention and intrusion in our lives that result from unnecessary and excessive growth of government. Ronald W. Reagan, "Inaugural Address, January 20, 1981," *Public Papers of the Presidents of the United States: Ronald Reagan 1981* (Washington: GPO, 1982), 1-2.

Endnotes

(9) Republican Party, "Republican Party Platform of 1980."

(10) The Internal Revenue Service (IRS) had denied tax-exempt status to religious schools that it found had violated federal non-discrimination laws by admitting only white students. See Lugg, *For God and Country*, 84-89.

(11) The Republicans' education platform plank contrasted sharply with the Democrats'; the latter celebrated that "Federal aid to education has increased by 73 percent" and it promoted higher spending on a large number of other federal education programs. Democratic Party, "Democratic Party Platform of 1980," adopted August 13, 1980.

(12) Ronald F. Docksai, "The Department of Education," in Heritage Foundation, *Mandate for Leadership*, 163-197.

(13) For two histories on ED's establishment, see Robert Heffernan, *Cabinetmakers: Story of the Three-Year Battle to Establish the U.S. Department of Education* (Iuniverse, 2001); and Beryl A. Radin and Willis D. Hawley, *Politics of Federal Reorganization: Creating the U.S. Department of Education* (Pergamon Books Inc., 1988)

(14) The NEA encouraged this view. For example, Ken Melley, an NEA spokesperson, told a reporter, "We endorsed Carter in 1976 on the basis of his campaign pledges. And he delivered on virtually every one of those promises: increased Federal funding for public education, the establishment of the Department of Education, opposition to the tuition tax credit program, support of the E.R.A. and human and civil rights." Leslie Bennetts, "Teachers Show Their Strength at Garden," *New York Times*, August 14, 1980, p. B3.

(15) These claims cannot be dismissed as groundless; the federal government has and still does fund much research into curricula. In some instances, the curricula produced have promoted educational ideas that are of questionable efficacy and offensive to many parents. Perhaps the best known is "Man: A Course of Study" (MACOS) a social studies

curriculum developed by the Educational Development Center, Inc., a not-for-profit that has produced curricular materials on child development, gender equity, cross-cultural understanding, health promotion, and more. MACOS was federally funded and adopted by many schools. The curriculum directed children to look to other cultures and use reason to come to their own conclusions about the nature of man and ethical issues, even on such politically sensitive issues such as euthanasia and abortion. Conservatives' distrust of federal bureaucrats forcing offensive curricula on the schools goes back many decades. For example, in 1950, a pamphlet written by the Federal Security Administration appeared to urge public schools to teach sexual education. A tempest arose in Congress and President Harry S. Truman was required to enter the fray and clarify that the pamphlet was not urging what critics imagined. Gilbert E. Smith, *The Limits of Reform: Politics and Federal Aid to Education, 1937-1950* (Garland Publishing Company, 1982), 209.

(16) Inflation rates from 1979 to 1983 were, respectively, 11.3, 13.5, 10.3, 6.3, and 3.2 percent.

(17) Barry Sussmann, "Reagan Program Strongly Backed," *Washington Post*, February 24, 1981. President Carter, in his FY1982 budget requested nearly $809.8 billion in federal budget authority. Reagan, by January of 1982, estimated that he had reduced this amount to $765.5 billion. Office of Management and Budget, *The Budget of the United States Government 1982* (Washington: GPO, 1981, 1982) 9.

(18) Office of Management and Budget, *Fiscal Year 1982 Budget Revisions* (Washington: OMB, March 1981), M-1. For simplicity's sake, this study refers to federal budgets in simple year format (e.g., "1982," 1983," etc.) instead of fiscal years ("FY1982, FY1983," etc.).

(19) Stockman, *The Triumph of Politics*, 318. This stands in sharp contrast to President Carter's proposal, which would have boosted the budget authority of the Department of Education by 15.5 percent or $2.3 billion. Angela Evans, "Overview and Analysis of the Reagan Administration's Budget Requests for Programs Administered by the

Department of Education, Fiscal Years 1982 Through 1984," report, Congressional Research Service, 1983, 5.

(20) Evans, *Overview and Analysis of the Regan Administration's Budget Requests for Programs Administered by the Department of Education, Fiscal Years 1982 Through 1984*, 15-16.

(21) For one perspective on this process, see Stockman, *The Triumph of Politics*.

(22) Bell attributed that description to Chief of Staff, Edward Meese. See Bell, *The Thirteenth Man*, p. 2.

(23) Ronald W. Reagan, "Address to the Nation on the program for Economic recovery, September 24, 1981," and "Remarks and a Question-and-Answer Session at a Working Luncheon With Out-of-town Editors," *Public Papers of the Presidents of the United States: Ronald Reagan, 1981* (Washington: GPO: 1982), 833, 958, and 959.

(24) Congressional Quarterly, *CQ Almanacs 1981-1983* (CQ, 1982-1984).

(25) Office of Management and Budget, The *Budget of the United States Government, Fiscal Year 1983* (Washington: OMB, 1982), 5-106 and 5-108.

(26) Garrison Nelson with Clark H. Bensen, *Committees in the U.S. Congress 1947-1992* (Washington: CQ Press, 1993), 465.

(27) In the U.S., a great portion of school funding comes from property taxes levied by local governments. In poor areas, property values tend to be low and, correspondingly, the schools funds derived from property low.

(28) Bell, *The Thirteenth Man*, p. 2.

(29) Ibid., 115.

(30) Eileen White and Jeffrey Mervis, "In Letters to Stockman, Bell Protests Education Cuts," *Education Week*, November 2, 1981.

(31)) Bell, *The Thirteenth Man*, 116.

(32) National Commission on Educational Excellence, *A Nation At Risk: The Imperative for Educational Reform*, (Washington: GPO, 1983), 5.

(33) Ronald W. Reagan, "Interview with USA Today, April 27, 1983," *Weekly Compilation of Presidential Documents*, May 2, 1983, vol. 19, no. 17, 596.

(34) Ronald W. Reagan, "Remarks on Receiving the Final Report of the National Commission on Excellence in Education, April 26, 1983," *Public Papers of the Presidents of the United States: Ronald Reagan, 1983*, book 1 (Washington: GPO, 1984), 585.

(35) Thomas Ferraro, "Panel Backs More — and Harder — School Work," *Universal Press International*, April 27, 1983.

(36) Dick Kirschten, "The Politics of Education," *National Journal*, July 9, 1983, 1448.

(37) Thomas Ferraro, "The Sorry State of U.S. Schools," *Universal Press International*, May 25, 1983. *A Nation at Risk* was followed immediately by reports and studies by the Education Commission of the States, the Business-Higher Education Forum, the Twentieth Century Fund, the National Science Board, and others. All of them concluded that schools were not educating children as well as they should and that the federal government could make policy to contend with it. Reports include: The Task Force on Education for Economic Growth of the Education Commission of the States, *Action for Excellence*; Business-Higher Education Forum, *America's Competitive Challenge*; Twentieth Century Fund Task Force on Elementary and Secondary Education Policy, *Making the Grade*; National Science Board Commission on Precollege Education in Mathematics, Science, and Technology, *Educating Americans for the*

21st Century. As quoted in John Brademas, *The Politics of Education: Conflict and Consensus on Capitol Hill* (University of Oklahoma Press, 1987), 63-65.

(38) Hendrick Smith, *The Power Game: How Washington Works* (Ballantine Books, 1988), 412.

(39) Kirschten, "The Politics of Education," 1448.

(40) Thomas Ferraro, "Untitled Newswire," *United Press International*, June 7, 1983. Bell said David Stockman of OMB backed off further cutting the Department of Education's budget. Politically, education had become a "sensitive issue." Bell, *The Thirteenth Man*, p. 131. Just a day earlier, though, Reagan reaffirmed his desire to abolish the Department of Education. Ferraro, "Senate Proposal for National Education Conference," *United Press International*, June 6, 1983.

(41) Edward Fiske, "Top Objectives Elude Reagan As Education Policy Evolves," *New York Times,* December 27, 1983, A1.

(42) One White House aide said that education had become a "dynamite issue that has sent an early surge of adrenaline into the nascent 1984 campaign." Kirschten, "The Politics of Education," 1448.

(43) William J. Bennett, *First Lessons: A Report on Elementary Education in America* (Washington: GPO, 1986); William J. Bennett, *American Education: Making It Work* (Washington: GPO, 1988); and William J. Bennett, *Our Children and Our Country: Affirming the Common Culture* (Simon & Schuster, 1988).

(44) Bennett, *American Education*, 232.

(45) Preamble, *The Constitution of the United States of America* and The Federalist Papers #10 and #47.

(46) "Remarks on Receiving the Final Report of the National Commission on Excellence in Education, April 26, 1983," *Public Papers of the Presidents of the United States: Ronald Reagan,* 1983, 586.

(47) Kirschten, "The Politics of Education," 1447.

(48) Richard G. Niemi et. al., *Trends in Public Opinion: A Compendium of Survey Data* (Greenwood Press, 1989), 84. In 1973, 49 percent of the public wanted to spend more for education and 47 percent wanted it to stay the same or reduce it. Come 1988, 64 percent favored increased spending on education and 33 percent thought otherwise. William G. Mayer, *The Changing American Mind: How and Why American Public Opinion Changed Between 1960 and 1988* (University of Michigan Press, 1993), 86.

(49) Dick M. Carpenter II, "Ronald Reagan and the Redefinition of the 'Education President,'" *Texas Education Review*, winter 2003-2004.

(50) Congressional Quarterly, *CQ Almanac 1985* (Washington: CQ, 1986), 293.

(51) Ibid.

(52) Lacking a line item veto, Reagan could not pick which federal programs he wanted to support. Once Congress sent him an education spending bill, he had to sign it in its entirety or veto the whole of it.

(53) The term "education outlays" refers to expenditures by the Department of Education. As such, these figures do include funds spent by other federal agencies on educational programs.

(54) In order to compute the agency outlays for the Department of Education before its start in 1980, OMB took the current array of programs and administrative structures as the Department's "agency structure," then compiled all figures for these programs and structures for

each year back to 1962. See *Budget of the United States Government, Fiscal Year 2010: Historical Tables*, p. 13.

(55) On presidents and education from 1980 to 2002, see Kevin R. Kosar, *Failing Grades: The Federal Politics of Education Standards* (Lynne Rienner Publishers, 2005), chapters 3-6; and Patrick J. McGuinn, *No Child Left Behind and the Transformation of Federal Education Policy* (University Press of Kansas, 2006), chapters 3-8.

(56) Kosar, *Failng Grades*, 185-186.

(57) On the No Child Left Behind Act of 2001 (P.L. 107-110), see Ibid., chapter 6.

Suggested Readings and Resources

Articles and Books

Terrel Bell, *The Thirteenth Man: A Reagan Cabinet Memoir* (Free Press, 1988)

Christopher T. Cross, *Political Education: National Policy Comes of Age* (Teachers College Press, 2003), chapter 5

Gareth Davies, *See Government Grow: Education Politics from Johnson to Reagan* (University of Kansas Press, 2007), chapter 10

Chester E. Finn, Jr., "The Disassembly of the Federal Educational Role," *Education and Urban Society*, May 1983

Chester E. Finn, Jr., "Education Policy and the Reagan Administration: A Large but Incomplete Success," *Educational Policy*, December 1988

National Commission on Educational Excellence, *A Nation At Risk: The Imperative for Educational Reform* (Washington: GPO, 1983).

Robert V. Heffernan, *Cabinetmakers: Story of the Three-Year Battle to Establish the U.S. Department of Education* (Iuniverse, 2001)

Beryl A. Radin and Willis D. Hawley, *Politics of Federal Reorganization: Creating the U.S. Department of Education* (Pergamon Books Inc., 1988)

Suggested Readings and Resources

Websites

The Federal Education Policy History website
http://federaleducationpolicy.wordpress.com/

U.S. Department of Education website
http://www.ed.gov

About the Author

Kevin R. Kosar is the author of *Failing Grades: The Federal Politics of Education Standards*, and the editor of *Bridging the Gap: Higher Education and Career-Centered Welfare Reform*. He created the Federal Education Policy History website, a free, nonpartisan educational resource.

Kosar has served as a peer-reviewer for the U.S. Department of Education's Teaching American History Grant Program and Presidential Academies for American History and Civics programs.

His writings have appeared in scholarly and professional journals, such as *Presidential Studies Quarterly*, *Public Administration Review*, and *Teachers College Record*; and in popular media, including *The Weekly Standard* magazine, the *Chicago Sun-Times*, *New York Press*, and *Philadelphia Inquirer* newspapers, and online publications, such as *History News Network*.

www.ingramcontent.com/pod-product-compliance
Lightning Source LLC
Chambersburg PA
CBHW060658280326
41933CB00012B/2228